※ Smithsonian

LITTLE EXPLORER

SPACE FLIGHTS

by Kathryn Clay

raintree

a Capstone company — publishers for children

Raintree is an imprint of Capstone Global Library Limited, a company incorporated in England and Wales having its registered office at 264 Banbury Road, Oxford, OX2 7DY – Registered company number: 6695582

www.raintree.co.uk
myorders@raintree.co.uk

ISBN 978 1 4747 3302 1
21 20 19 18 17
10 9 8 7 6 5 4 3 2 1

British Library Cataloguing in Publication Data
A full catalogue record for this book is available from the British Library.

Editorial Credits
Arnold Ringstad, editor; Laura Polzin, designer and production specialist

Our very special thanks to Dr. Valerie Neal, Curator and Chair of the Space History Department at the Smithsonian National Air and Space Museum for her curatorial review. Capstone would also like to thank Kealy Gordon, Smithsonian Institution Product Development Manager, and the following at Smithsonian Enterprises: Christopher A. Liedel, President; Carol LeBlanc, Senior Vice President; Brigid Ferraro, Vice President; Ellen Nanney, Licensing Manager.

Acknowledgements
Getty Images: Hulton Archives/Keystone, 19, UIG/Sovfoto, 18, 26; NASA: cover, 1, 3, 6 (background), 6 (foreground), 7, 8, 9 (left), 9 (right), 13, 14, 15 (bottom), 16 (background), 16 (foreground), 17, 20, 21, 23, 25 (top), 25 (bottom), 27, 28, 29 (top), 29 (bottom), 30–31; Science Source, 4, 24, RIA Novosti, 5 (top), 10, 11, 12; Shutterstock: pockygallery, 15 (top)

Design Elements: Shutterstock Images: Antares_StarExplorer, MarcelClemens, Ovchinnkov Vladimir, pio3, Shay Yacobinski, Tashal, Teneresa

Printed and bound in China.

CONTENTS

THE FIRST PERSON IN SPACE

On 12 April 1961 the
Soviet Union launched
a rocket into space. At the
rocket's top was a small
spacecraft. Cosmonaut
Yuri Gagarin was inside.
He became the first
person in space.

The Soviet Union later
split into several countries,
including Russia.

Gagarin's launch

Gagarin was in space for 108 minutes. He circled the planet once. Then he returned to Earth. His mission paved the way for many amazing space flights.

Yuri Gagarin

Astronauts from 40 countries have flown in space.

MAJOR SPACE FLIGHTS

mission name	launch date	accomplishments	country
Vostok 1	12 April 1961	first person in space	Soviet Union
Gemini 8	16 March 1966	first docking	United States
Apollo 11	16 July 1969	first moon landing	United States
Soyuz 11	6 June 1971	first space station boarding	Soviet Union
STS-1	12 April 1981	first space shuttle flight	United States
STS-135	8 July 2011	last space shuttle flight	United States

THE FIRST AMERICAN IN SPACE

NASA soon sent the first American astronaut into space. On 5 May 1961, Astronaut Alan Shepard flew into space in a small capsule. It was called *Freedom 7*.

Alan Shepard

NASA stands for National Aeronautics and Space Administration. It is the United States' space agency.

Shepard did not circle Earth. Instead, he flew up to a height of 187 kilometres (116 miles), then came straight down again. His space flight lasted about 15 minutes.

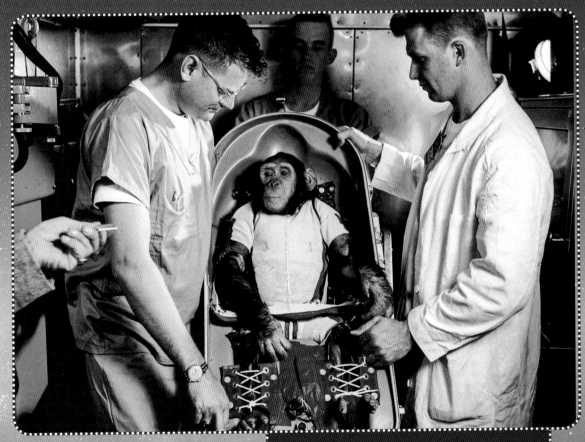

A chimpanzee named Ham flew on the flight before Shepard's mission.

JOHN GLENN'S HISTORIC FLIGHT

John Glenn became the first American to orbit Earth. His capsule, *Friendship 7*, launched from Florida, U.S.A. on 20 February 1962. Glenn circled Earth three times. He spent about five hours in space.

Glenn climbs into his spacecraft.

Glenn was a national hero. People in New York City celebrated his space flight with a parade. Cities named schools and streets after him.

Glenn in 1962

Glenn in 1998

Glenn flew into space again 36 years later. He joined six other astronauts on a winged spacecraft called a space shuttle in 1998. At 77 years old, he was the oldest astronaut ever.

THE FIRST WOMAN IN SPACE

The first woman to fly in space was Valentina Tereshkova. She was an experienced parachutist from the Soviet Union.

Tereshkova (left) had experience parachuting from planes.

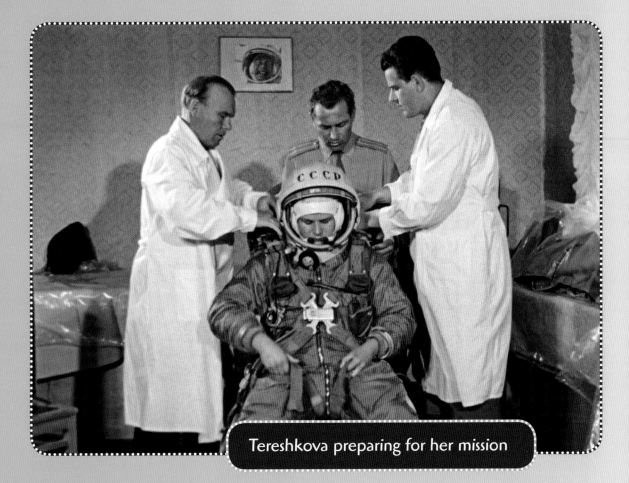

Tereshkova preparing for her mission

Tereshkova flew on the Vostok 6 mission. Her mission began on 16 June 1963. She circled the planet 48 times in nearly 71 hours.

It was 19 years before another woman went into space. Cosmonaut Svetlana Savitskaya flew in August 1982.

THE FIRST SPACEWALK

When a person exits a spacecraft in space, it is called a spacewalk. Russian Cosmonaut Alexei Leonov was the first person to go on a spacewalk. On 18 March 1965, he spent 10 minutes floating outside his ship. He stayed connected to the ship by a tether.

A few months later, Ed White became the first American astronaut to go on a spacewalk. He did this on the Gemini 4 mission. White also used a tether so he would not float away from his ship.

tether

Ed White

ORBITING THE MOON

On 24 December 1968, the Apollo 8 mission orbited the moon. U.S. Astronauts Frank Borman, Jim Lovell and Bill Anders were on board. They were the first people to go so far away from Earth. They watched their home planet rise over the moon's horizon. They returned safely to Earth a few days later.

NASA prepared for a moon landing. The astronauts on the Apollo 9 and Apollo 10 missions tested their spacecraft. They practised the steps they would need to land. They hoped their planning would pay off.

The Apollo 8 astronauts took photos of Earth rising.

APOLLO 8 FLIGHT PATH

(distances not to scale)

LUNAR ORBIT

When a spacecraft is circling the moon, it is said to be in lunar orbit. On the Apollo 8 mission, the astronauts orbited the moon 10 times before returning home.

LANDING

LAUNCH

THE MOON LANDING

On 20 July 1969, the three astronauts of the Apollo 11 mission launched to the moon. They were Neil Armstrong, Buzz Aldrin and Michael Collins.

Michael Collins

Buzz Aldrin

Neil Armstrong

Apollo 11 lifted off from Florida.

Armstrong and Aldrin took the lander down to the moon's surface. Collins waited in the main spacecraft in lunar orbit. Armstrong and Aldrin exited the lander and walked around. They collected rocks and soil to study. They took photos. A few days later, all three men returned to Earth.

lunar module

Buzz Aldrin

The astronauts set up science experiments on the surface of the moon.

THE FIRST SPACE STATION

The Soviet Union launched the first space station on 19 April 1971. It was named Salyut 1. The station did not have anyone travelling inside.

inside the Salyut 1 space station

The crew of the Soyuz 11 mission flew to the station in June 1971. They stayed aboard for 23 days. Sadly all three crew members died. The air leaked out of their spacecraft as they returned to Earth. The cosmonauts didn't have enough oxygen to survive.

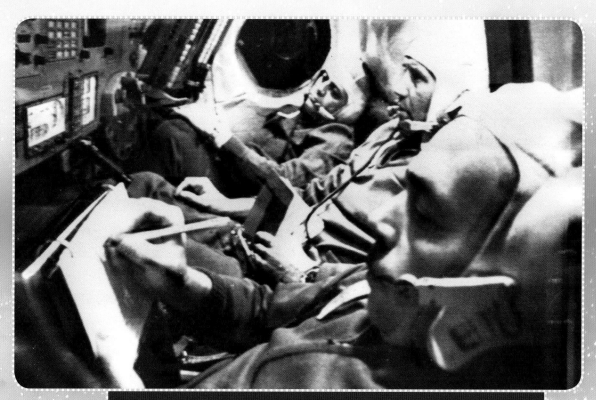

The Soyuz 11 crew included Vladislav Volkov (left), Viktor Patsayev (middle) and Georgi Dobrovolski (right).

INTERNATIONAL SPACE STATION

The largest space station ever built is the International Space Station (ISS). It usually holds six people at a time.

THE SPACE SHUTTLE

The space shuttle was the first reusable spacecraft. It could return to Earth, then be launched into space again. There have been five space shuttles. They were named *Columbia, Challenger, Discovery, Atlantis* and *Endeavour*.

fuel tank

space shuttle orbiter

solid rocket boosters

The first shuttle launched on 12 April 1981.
Columbia took off from Florida, U.S.A.
U.S. Astronauts John Young and Bob Crippen
flew the ship. The men circled Earth 36 times.
They landed the ship in the California desert like
an aeroplane.

the space shuttle
Columbia landing

THE FIRST AMERICAN WOMAN IN SPACE

In 1977 Sally Ride answered a newspaper advertisement from NASA. The space agency was looking for more astronauts. About 8,000 people applied. Ride was one of 35 who were chosen.

On 18 June 1983, she became the first American woman in space. Ride flew on the space shuttle *Challenger*. She carried out science experiments in space. She inspired many girls and women.

TIMELINE: WOMEN IN SPACE

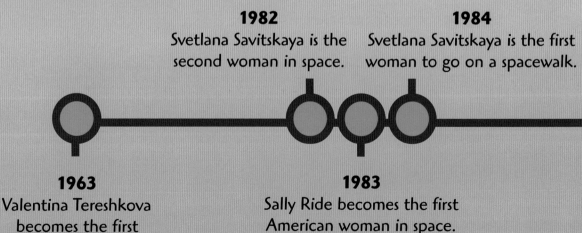

1982
Svetlana Savitskaya is the second woman in space.

1984
Svetlana Savitskaya is the first woman to go on a spacewalk.

1963
Valentina Tereshkova becomes the first woman in space.

1983
Sally Ride becomes the first American woman in space.

"I didn't really decide that I wanted to be an astronaut for sure until the end of college. But even in elementary school and junior high, I was very interested in space and in the space programme."
—Sally Ride

1995
Eileen Collins is the first American woman to pilot a spacecraft.

1992
Mae Jemison becomes the first African–American woman in space.

1999
Eileen Collins is the first woman to command a U.S. space mission.

SPACE DISASTERS

The space shuttle programme suffered two major disasters. The first came in 1986. On 28 January seven astronauts boarded *Challenger*. Just 73 seconds after liftoff, an explosion destroyed the shuttle. All seven astronauts died.

Challenger is destroyed during launch.

Another tragedy happened in 2003. The shuttle *Columbia* broke apart as it returned to Earth on 1 February. All seven crew members died. After disaster, NASA studied what went wrong. It made changes to make future space missions safer.

the crew of *Challenger*

the crew of *Columbia*

BRITONS IN SPACE

Astronaut Helen Sharman launched into space on board a Soviet spacecraft in 1991. She became the first British citizen to travel into space. British companies helped pay for her trip. Sharman spent eight days on the Mir space station.

Helen Sharman

People born in the U.K. had flown into space before. However, they became U.S. citizens before flying with NASA.

The European Space Agency (ESA) trains astronauts from Europe to fly in space. The first British ESA astronaut was Tim Peake. He flew into space on 15 December 2015.

Tim Peake

FUTURE SPACE FLIGHTS

There are exciting missions ahead for NASA. The agency is building a new spacecraft called Orion. It will carry four astronauts into space. It may travel to the moon, to asteroids or to Mars.

ORION
SPACECRAFT

Businesses are working on space travel, too. SpaceX has a spacecraft called Dragon. Orbital ATK has one called Cygnus. Both have carried supplies to the ISS. These and other companies plan to make space flights easier and cheaper. More people will be able to go on space flights than ever before.

DRAGON
SPACECRAFT

CYGNUS
SPACECRAFT

GLOSSARY

asteroid rock that drifts through space

capsule small spacecraft that holds astronauts and other travellers

cosmonaut Russian astronaut

disaster sudden event that causes damage or loss of life

docking connecting with another spacecraft in space

lander spacecraft designed to safely land on a moon or planet

orbit curved path of a spacecraft around an object in space

parachutist person who jumps out of aircraft with a parachute

spacewalk leaving a spacecraft or space station to work outside

tether rope or cord that connects two objects together

tragedy event causing suffering and sadness

COMPREHENSION QUESTIONS

1. Where are some places that future space flights might go?

2. How did the first U.S. flight differ from the first Soviet flight?

3. Pages 16 and 17 discuss the first moon landing. Based on this description, would you want to walk on the moon, like Armstrong and Aldrin, or stay in the orbiting spacecraft, like Collins?

READ MORE

Astronauts Explore the Galaxy (Launch Into Space!), Carmen Bredeson and Indra Vathryn (Enslow Publishing, 2015).

Everything Space (National Geographic Kids, 2015).

Space Pioneers (Story of Space), Steve Parker (Smart Apple Media, 2016).

WEBSITES

BBC: Apollo 11
www.bbc.co.uk/science/space/solarsystem/space_missions/ apollo_11
Explore the first moon landing.

BBC: Space Flight Timeline
news.bbc.co.uk/2/hi/science/nature/6996121.stm
Learn about important dates in the history of space flight.

ESA
www.esa.int/esaKIDSen/SEMHNTRZ5BG_index_0.html
Read more about the ESA, which operates European space flights.

INDEX